Speak Positive Get Positive!

Speak Negative Get Negative!

Vol 1

TODD RAY ABERNATHY

Speak Positive...Get Positive!
Speak Negative...Get Negative!
ISBN: 0-88144-302-6
Copyright © 2008 by Todd Ray Abernathy

Published by
Victory Graphics and Media
9731 East 54th Street
Tulsa, OK 74146
www.victorygraphicsandmedia.com

Printed in the United States of America. All rights reserved under International Copyright Law. No part of this book may be reproduced or transmitted in any form or by any means, electronic or mechanical, including photocopying, recording, or by any information storage and retrieval system without permission in writing from the publisher.

INTRODUCTION

Hi, my name is Todd Ray Abernathy. Thank you for purchasing this book of my personal quotations.

In this book you'll find my own personal mottos that have helped me over come my own negative ways of speaking and thinking. I had to teach myself a different way of thinking from how I was taught by other people growing up.

Any person can change their negative thinking and turn it into positive thinking over time. By reading this book it will give you the courage to turn negative thinking into positive thinking just as these quotes have helped me improve my life.

I dedicate this book to YOU for taking action in improving your life for the better and to my best friend Tracy Nicole Abernathy who is my life partner and my inspiration.

CONTENTS

PART 1　Business Inspiration 7

PART 2　Family Inspiration 37

PART 3　Financial Inspiration 45

PART 4　Personal Inspiration 75

PART 5　Spiritual Inspiration 129

PART 6　Success Inspiration 155

PART 1

Business Inspiration

Problem solving starts by giving yourself more than one solution.

TODD RAY ABERNATHY

Stick with
your goals,
because only
you know how
important your
goals are.

TODD RAY ABERNATHY

You may get
one hundred no's,
but it only takes
one yes.

TODD RAY ABERNATHY

Learn from your mistake and move on.

TODD RAY ABERNATHY

You always
have the option
to renegotiate
a better deal.

TODD RAY ABERNATHY

Become a problem solver.

TODD RAY ABERNATHY

One sale is
great, two
is even better.

TODD RAY ABERNATHY

In business,
time is your enemy.
Do what it takes
to show a profit as
soon as possible.

TODD RAY ABERNATHY

If you never
take a risk you'll
never gain.

TODD RAY ABERNATHY

If you never take
a risk you'll never
reach as high
as you can.

TODD RAY ABERNATHY

The title is what makes people look inside.

TODD RAY ABERNATHY

Most stores
never have what
you want, only
what they want
you to have.
Be different and
fill want list.

TODD RAY ABERNATHY

See
opportunity
where
others don't.

TODD RAY ABERNATHY

Sometimes it's
best to turn down
a deal, so you
can be in control
of the product.

TODD RAY ABERNATHY

People,
equal money.
The more people
that you reach
the more money
you'll make.

TODD RAY ABERNATHY

When the money is in your hand, that's when you know it's guaranteed.

TODD RAY ABERNATHY

When you can't get it all done, it's time for you to outsource.

TODD RAY ABERNATHY

By studying all
of your options,
you can take an
educated risk
instead of an
uneducated risk.

TODD RAY ABERNATHY

Show your employees that you care and they'll stay with your company longer.

TODD RAY ABERNATHY

Ask your
employees how
to improve your
company and the
information that you
get will increase
your company's
profit margin.

TODD RAY ABERNATHY

When you decide
to work for yourself,
stay at your current job
until you're making
more money working
for yourself, only then
should you quit
your current job.

TODD RAY ABERNATHY

The best sales people in the world don't try to sell, they help you solve your problem.

TODD RAY ABERNATHY

Give your customers instant benefits and they will always buy from you.

TODD RAY ABERNATHY

Choose a
business that
you love and
you'll feel like the
person you were
meant to be.

TODD RAY ABERNATHY

To succeed in
your business
you must have
all three plans;
a business plan,
a marketing plan
and
a financial plan.

TODD RAY ABERNATHY

Don't look at
your competitor
as competition,
but rather as
someone who
is helping you
make your business
even better.

TODD RAY ABERNATHY

Don't have the misconception that a business will run itself.

TODD RAY ABERNATHY

Don't invest in
a business that
is controlled by
the economy.

TODD RAY ABERNATHY

PART 2

Family Inspiration

Your children
can be your
biggest asset,
if you choose
to encourage
your children to
follow their dreams
and goals.

TODD RAY ABERNATHY

Become the type of parent that works with your children and their ideas.

TODD RAY ABERNATHY

Marry your
best friend and
you know you'll
be with someone
you love.

TODD RAY ABERNATHY

GOD gives
special parents,
special children.

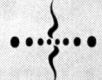

TODD RAY ABERNATHY

Positive communication will keep your marriage intact.

TODD RAY ABERNATHY

Enjoy life by
making time for
the silly things.

TODD RAY ABERNATHY

Don't jump into
a relationship
before becoming
best friends.

TODD RAY ABERNATHY

PART 3

Financial Inspiration

There are two types of people, poor thinkers and wealthy thinkers.

TODD RAY ABERNATHY

A wise person saves their money.

TODD RAY ABERNATHY

Investing in
a person is the
best investment
that you can make.

TODD RAY ABERNATHY

Tax the wealthy and tax yourself out of a job.

TODD RAY ABERNATHY

Save twenty
percent of
your yearly
income for unseen
future set backs.

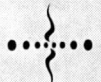

TODD RAY ABERNATHY

A sale is only
a sale if you
are already
buying.

TODD RAY ABERNATHY

With zero
business taxes
your community
will grow with
more businesses
and jobs.

TODD RAY ABERNATHY

Be thrifty,
not a
cheapskate.

TODD RAY ABERNATHY

Most wealthy
people started
out with a
small amount
of money and
one great ideal.

TODD RAY ABERNATHY

Taxes should
be raised
only through
sin taxes.

TODD RAY ABERNATHY

Save your
money during
the good times
because
you'll need it
for the bad times.

TODD RAY ABERNATHY

Wealthy people
hire people
poor people
don't.

TODD RAY ABERNATHY

Assessor tax is; the elimination of private property. That's the same definition as communism.

TODD RAY ABERNATHY

Cash on hand,
is the most
important asset
that you
can have.

TODD RAY ABERNATHY

People always invest their money where their faith is.

TODD RAY ABERNATHY

An asset can
disappear over time.
Invest in more than
one asset and have
as many assets
working for you
at the same time.

TODD RAY ABERNATHY

Gambling is a liability, not an asset.

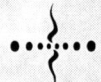

TODD RAY ABERNATHY

Sometimes GOD
humbles you
financially so
you can be brought
to the place in life
that you were
meant to be.

TODD RAY ABERNATHY

The reason you
take a job is for
the money, not for
the sake of having a job.
When you're looking
for a job, start with
the highest paying job
and work your way up.

TODD RAY ABERNATHY

Since a job is
a liability,
when you have
a job invest
your money
in things that
are assets.

TODD RAY ABERNATHY

Don't get so
caught up in
your job that
you can't focus
on your
future assets.

TODD RAY ABERNATHY

When a person gets greedy, that person will always end up with less in the long run.

TODD RAY ABERNATHY

The things that are given away for free, are the things that are going to cost you the most.

TODD RAY ABERNATHY

When you
work for a
big company,
asking and getting
what you want is
all about timing.

TODD RAY ABERNATHY

You are
worth more
than a job
could ever
pay you.

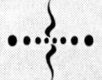

TODD RAY ABERNATHY

Don't talk
yourself into
being poor,
talk yourself into
being wealthy.

TODD RAY ABERNATHY

Invest your
off time
toward things
that are assets.

TODD RAY ABERNATHY

Think ahead,
people fail
their own future
by not
thinking ahead.

TODD RAY ABERNATHY

PART 4

Personal Inspiration

Don't let
other people's
words manipulate
your life.

TODD RAY ABERNATHY

Life is a journey of learning.

TODD RAY ABERNATHY

By helping a
homeless person,
you are saving your
own community.

TODD RAY ABERNATHY

Don't let
your mind limit
your abilities.

TODD RAY ABERNATHY

You can't base your life on a grade.

TODD RAY ABERNATHY

Before you
argue with
someone,
remember
you have
other options.

TODD RAY ABERNATHY

Tell the
positive side
of the story,
not just the
negative side.

TODD RAY ABERNATHY

Do not let laziness rule your life.

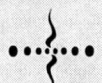

TODD RAY ABERNATHY

Learn how
to turn
the negatives
in your life
into positives.

TODD RAY ABERNATHY

When you
take advice from
a negative thinker
you will not live
your life to your
fullest potential.

TODD RAY ABERNATHY

Learning
is
never ending.

TODD RAY ABERNATHY

If you take
away one
person's rights,
you're taking
away your
own rights.

TODD RAY ABERNATHY

Don't give up
before you
even start.

TODD RAY ABERNATHY

Anything that
comes easy
isn't worth
having anyway.

TODD RAY ABERNATHY

When you do nothing you get nothing.

TODD RAY ABERNATHY

As long as
you say
you can't do it,
you won't do it.

TODD RAY ABERNATHY

There are
many ways
to get the
same results.

TODD RAY ABERNATHY

Yes!
You can do
what you
want to do
in life.

TODD RAY ABERNATHY

Nobody sees
the vision
until it's
staring them
in the face.

TODD RAY ABERNATHY

Speak positive
get positive!
Speak negative
get negative!

TODD RAY ABERNATHY

There are no
guarantees in life,
you only have
right now.

TODD RAY ABERNATHY

If you come
across as
desperate,
you'll be treated
as desperate.

TODD RAY ABERNATHY

By running
from your fear
and not facing it,
you'll always
be running.

TODD RAY ABERNATHY

Don't criticize
others when
you're not
in their shoes.

TODD RAY ABERNATHY

To receive less criticism from others, don't tell everything to everybody.

TODD RAY ABERNATHY

Stop your
addiction or
it will sidetrack
your direction
in life.

TODD RAY ABERNATHY

You can never please a negative thinker.

TODD RAY ABERNATHY

If someone
tells you that
they know it all,
run from them
as fast as
you can.

TODD RAY ABERNATHY

By not choosing, is choosing.

TODD RAY ABERNATHY

We each have
a special gift
and to use
your gift,
you first have
to be happy
with yourself.

TODD RAY ABERNATHY

When you
go to an all you
can eat buffet,
don't eat
all you can eat.

TODD RAY ABERNATHY

Retirement doesn't mean that you're dead. Make your last days count.

TODD RAY ABERNATHY

When another
person uses
angry words,
nod and say nothing.
Then that person
will realize what
they have said
was wrong.

TODD RAY ABERNATHY

Your actions
show the world
who you
really are.

TODD RAY ABERNATHY

Sometimes we
don't see
ourselves
until someone
points it out.

TODD RAY ABERNATHY

Only you
can see your
true destiny.

TODD RAY ABERNATHY

It's only as hard as you make it.

TODD RAY ABERNATHY

Don't let
someone else's
fear become
your fear.

TODD RAY ABERNATHY

People always
appreciate
being
appreciated.

TODD RAY ABERNATHY

A wealthy thinker always values their time.

TODD RAY ABERNATHY

Complaining
is a waste
of time
and energy.

TODD RAY ABERNATHY

Apologizing
for someone else's
rude behavior
only allows
a rude person
to continue
to be rude.

TODD RAY ABERNATHY

Most government politicians think that it's there job to have continual growth in spending and it's the people's job to stop government's wasteful spending.

TODD RAY ABERNATHY

Follow the
same rules
that you make
for others.

TODD RAY ABERNATHY

Your life
is unique,
don't compare
your life
to other
people's lives.

TODD RAY ABERNATHY

It's better
to work
for yourself,
than to
work a job.

TODD RAY ABERNATHY

A true friend
is someone
who goes out
of their way
when there's
nothing in it
for them.

TODD RAY ABERNATHY

Don't let
other people's
comments
reflect on you.

TODD RAY ABERNATHY

Those who
tell everything
to everybody,
can loose
everything that's
important.

TODD RAY ABERNATHY

For a great
way of life,
eat healthy, exercise,
stay away from
junk food and
you won't have to
worry about the
weight on a scale.

TODD RAY ABERNATHY

Those who
carry pen
and paper
will be able to
accomplish
great things.

TODD RAY ABERNATHY

As you
get older,
remember
that you're
not alone.

TODD RAY ABERNATHY

Games are
fun, turn
your work
into a game.

TODD RAY ABERNATHY

PART 5

Spiritual Inspiration

Keep your spiritual guard up at all times.

TODD RAY ABERNATHY

If you
want peace,
you must
become
a peacemaker.

TODD RAY ABERNATHY

Worship GOD not religion.

TODD RAY ABERNATHY

Being a
peacemaker
doesn't mean
that you have to
let other people
take advantage of
you continuously.

TODD RAY ABERNATHY

Trust in GOD
and everything
will fall
into place.

TODD RAY ABERNATHY

Look at
everything
in your life
as a blessing.

TODD RAY ABERNATHY

Give love, compassion and positive education to the incarcerated and they will give back love and compassion to society. Give hate and no compassion to the incarcerated and they will give back total anarchy to society.

TODD RAY ABERNATHY

Through prayer,
is where GOD
gives you
your strength.

TODD RAY ABERNATHY

Be aware of
people that prey
upon your kindness,
for they see it
as a weakness and
know that your
kindness is your
greatest strength.

TODD RAY ABERNATHY

Love always
wins in
the end.

TODD RAY ABERNATHY

Don't expect
compassion,
if you yourself
are not
compassionate
to others.

TODD RAY ABERNATHY

Some people
are blessed
with a great gift
and they refuse
to use it.

TODD RAY ABERNATHY

You'll get
seven times back
from how you
treat others.

TODD RAY ABERNATHY

Let GOD
rule your life
not religion.

TODD RAY ABERNATHY

In heaven
there are many
beautiful souls
that have gone
before you and
they're waiting
there with love
to greet you.

TODD RAY ABERNATHY

Be careful
what you pray for,
because GOD
does deliver.

TODD RAY ABERNATHY

Thank you
GOD for letting
me be a light
for other people
in an otherwise
dark and
lonely world.

TODD RAY ABERNATHY

It's not the
money that's evil,
it's a person's greed
that's evil.

TODD RAY ABERNATHY

Our
disappointments
in life,
is GOD's way
of giving us a
promotion in life.

TODD RAY ABERNATHY

Sometimes
GOD will bring
a negative person
in your life,
just to show you
what not to
do with your life

TODD RAY ABERNATHY

When you dwell
on the past,
you won't see
what GOD
has for you
right now.

TODD RAY ABERNATHY

Let GOD
take away
all of your
worries and fears,
no matter
what they are.

TODD RAY ABERNATHY

As new people cross your path, thank GOD for bringing each person to you.

TODD RAY ABERNATHY

GOD brought
you to me,
when I needed
you the most.

TODD RAY ABERNATHY

The spiritual enemy can paint a pretty picture.

TODD RAY ABERNATHY

PART 6

Success Inspiration

Be yourself
and you'll
inspire others
to do the same.

TODD RAY ABERNATHY

Don't let
poor thinkers,
talk you out of
your dreams
and visions.

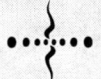

TODD RAY ABERNATHY

Sometimes
you have
to say no,
even when
you're desperate.

TODD RAY ABERNATHY

When you're
struggling,
is when you
learn the most.

TODD RAY ABERNATHY

When you're struggling, that's when you're at the most creative point in your life.

TODD RAY ABERNATHY

The use of
a person's name
is a very powerful
tool and the secret
to success is
knowing and using
everyone's name.

TODD RAY ABERNATHY

You'll get further in life by being yourself, than by being any other person.

TODD RAY ABERNATHY

You make the outcome of every situation.

TODD RAY ABERNATHY

Everyone's
version of
success
is different.

TODD RAY ABERNATHY

Say the wrong
words and you
won't get what
you want.
Say the right words
and you will get
what you want.

TODD RAY ABERNATHY

To write at
your best,
you have to
live it first.

TODD RAY ABERNATHY

You already
know what
the problem is,
find the solution
to solve
the problem.

TODD RAY ABERNATHY

Don't let your desire to be entertained steal all of your creative time.

TODD RAY ABERNATHY

Success is
achieved by being
in control of
your own product.

TODD RAY ABERNATHY

Successful people
don't make excuses,
they value other
people's time.

TODD RAY ABERNATHY

You'll accomplish
more by not
worrying what
other people think.

TODD RAY ABERNATHY

See everything
as having
unlimited
opportunity.

TODD RAY ABERNATHY

You can't have success without the work.

TODD RAY ABERNATHY

You can make
anything happen,
by having the
desire to make
it happen.

TODD RAY ABERNATHY

Success is teaming up with the right people.

TODD RAY ABERNATHY

You can invest your time in productive things or nonproductive things.

TODD RAY ABERNATHY

Trying is an accomplishment in it's self.

TODD RAY ABERNATHY

Take what
you've learned
from a mistake
and use it to
your advantage.

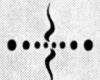

TODD RAY ABERNATHY

Everyone has
knowledge
that can help
another person.

TODD RAY ABERNATHY

Be a doer, not a complainer.

TODD RAY ABERNATHY

Write the best book that you can write and the rest will fall into place.

TODD RAY ABERNATHY

Hang around positive people and you'll reach your goals faster.

TODD RAY ABERNATHY

Help others
reach their goals
faster and you'll
be known as a
successful person.

TODD RAY ABERNATHY

Do your
own thing,
your own way
and you'll find
success faster.

TODD RAY ABERNATHY

An all voluntary military, is a strong military.

TODD RAY ABERNATHY

Always take advantage of what you're good at.

TODD RAY ABERNATHY

You can't do it all, pick one thing that you're great at and run with it.

TODD RAY ABERNATHY

If you never
give up
you'll never fail.

TODD RAY ABERNATHY

What good is money if you can't enjoy your life.

TODD RAY ABERNATHY

Don't focus on
what you can't do.
Focus on
what you can do.

TODD RAY ABERNATHY

Shoot for the best and let what happens happen.

TODD RAY ABERNATHY

CPSIA information can be obtained at www.ICGtesting.com
Printed in the USA
LVOW081432110412

277163LV00003B/244/P